T0157497

Expressions of My Heart

Collection of Poetry

AMANDA DAVENPORT

WESTBOW
PRESS®
A DIVISION OF THOMAS NELSON
& ZONDERVAN

WestBow Press books may be ordered through booksellers or by contacting:

WestBow Press
A Division of Thomas Nelson & Zondervan
1663 Liberty Drive
Bloomington, IN 47403
www.westbowpress.com
844-714-3454

Scripture quotations are taken from the Holy Bible, New International Version®, NIV®. Copyright © 1973, 1978, 1984 by Biblica, Inc.™ Used by permission of Zondervan. All rights reserved worldwide.

ISBN: 979-8-3850-1349-4 (sc)
ISBN: 979-8-3850-1350-0 (e)

Library of Congress Control Number: 2023922816

Print information available on the last page.

WestBow Press rev. date: 12/11/2023

CONTENTS

INTRODUCTION

"And we know that in all things God works for the good of those who love Him, who have been called according to His purpose." (Romans 8:28)

Expressions of my heart is a collection of poetry that God has inspired me through my experiences and His Word to share. This has been written over my lifetime starting at 18 years of age until the present time. I wrote these during seasons of revelation, pain, heartbreak, suffering, sorrow, tears, discouragement, peace, love, and truth. I hope as you read through these you are blessed, uplifted and inspired. I pray these poems draw you closer to God's word as you read through them.

God Bless,
Amanda

© Written by: Amanda Davenport

Baby Jesus

Three wise men went
Traveling by night
To see a baby named Jesus
Led by a star so bright

They found Him in a stable
Which the bright star had led
Sleeping in a manger where
He laid down His little head

Angels told country shepherds
"That a Savior is born this day
In the city of David"
Lying on a manger of hay

Shepherds then
Went from the fields to see
Little baby Jesus
Our Savior to be

The shepherds saw and made known
Of Christ Jesus birth
Who God sent to be a Savior
To everyone on earth

Inspired by Luke 2:1-20

My Savior

—·❧·—

"God so loved the world
That He gave His only son"
He who died to save
Each and everyone

Jesus died on the cross
For our sins to bear
For all who are lost
And those unaware

He loved the world so much
He even thought it worth
Experiencing heartache and pain
For sinners on this earth

He said "Father forgive them
For they know not what they do"
As they scoffed, and laughed
Yelling to Him, who are you?!

After He died He rose again
So everyone can have a choice
Whether or not to follow Him
To listen and obey His voice

When Jesus died for us
He gave the gift of love
That whosoever believes in Him
Will live forever up above

Inspired by John 3:16

God

The only God is three in one
Father, Spirit, and Son

When you call upon God's name
It will always stays the same

He will listen when you call
He will catch you when you fall

When you sin, He will forgive you
While you repent and forgive too

For when you make a mess
He doesn't love you less

He wraps you in His embrace
Always ready to give you grace

He says you're going to get through
Because He will walk with you

Because of what He's done
Through Jesus His Son
The battle is already won

The word of God always stands
He holds the world in His hands

He promises to give you more
Then you could ever ask for

You can't see Him, but He's there
He can be found everywhere

Inspired by Matthew 28:19

God's Friend

———◦✦◦———

God, I want to be a good friend to you
Living for you in everything I do

Though I don't always understand
I believe I'm held in Your hands

I love that I can tell you anything
Even though you already know everything

I want to help people to know you
By living out Your word that is true

I want to be a testimony of Your grace
By choosing to not give up on life's race

I want to avoid any type of temptation
"With you theres an escape in any situation"

I want to do whatever you say is right
You say "anything done in the dark will come to light"

I want to talk to you more
Please get into my core

You are my friend not my enemy
My enemy wants to destroy me,
But you always want to help me!

Inspired by 1 Corinthians 10:13

First Love

God, You'll always be my first love
One day I'll live forever up above

I will always keep You first in my life
Even when I'm married and I'm a wife

Your God and deserve to always be first
You're living water that satisfies my thirst

I'll also love You more than anybody on earth
For I respect Your sacred, honored worth

If I keep You first then all things will fall into place
Thank you so much for your undeserving grace

Your will for me has now become my lifestyle
Thinking of how You loved me first makes me smile

You loved me so much, Your Son died for my sins
Then "You choose to not remember them again"

Thank You for loving me, even when I couldn't love me
You promise in Your Word that You're love will always be

Inspired by John 4:14

Love Is

"Love is patient"
It doesn't expect everything to be urgent

"Love is kind"
It withstands the tests of time

"Love is not envious"
It's happy for other's success

"Love is not boastful"
It's being humble

"Love is not prideful"
It doesn't belittle people

"Love is not rude"
It doesn't seclude

"Love is not self-seeking"
It's compassionate and understanding

"Love is not easily angered"
It stays softly tempered

"Love keeps no record of wrongs done"
It forgives each and everyone

"Love is not delighted in evil"
It doesn't go down to the devil's level

"Love is truthful"
It's meaning is in the Bible

"'Love is protectful"
It's not hateful

"Love is trustworthy"
It gives faithfully

"Love is hopeful"
It has good expectations and is joyful

Inspired by 1 Corinthians 13:4-7

Have Hope

With God there's always hope
No matter the situation
He will help you cope

Even when times are bad
You don't have to act all sad

For hope says the future's bright
No matter your darkest night

He'll never steer you wrong
He'll help carry you along

Hope is a powerful word to say
It's the best way to pray

Hope

Hope is the attitude you need to show
Because God said "you reap what you sow"

You don't have to feel hope to have it
You just simply believe and never quit

Don't complain while you wait
Even if you don't feel great

Your atmosphere is affected by your attitude
So have a heart of renewed gratitude

Have God help you in everything you do
Don't expect for others to fix you

Hope and expect good things
Just see what hope brings

The most important part is not the wait
It's what you're doing while you wait
That determines your state

You can get what you expect
Give yourself that respect

God says consistency is the key
To keeping the victory

God says to put your hope in Him
Even when your life seems dim

God expects you to have faith and hope
While you're waiting, that's how you cope

Inspired by Galatians 6:8, Romans 8:25

Be Humble

God, here I am again at the place of brokenness
Let this place teach me humbleness

Help me learn that I really do need you
Not to judge because I'm a sinner too

When I'm wrong I should admit
Then to you humbly submit

You want me to be humble
You despise the prideful

Brokenness is good if I learn that when I stumble
That I still need to be humble

The bible says "pride cometh before a fall"
False pride is not being humbled at all

It is better to have an attitude of humbleness
Then let myself spoil from pridefulness

Inspired by Proverbs 16:18

I Still Love You

Have you ever wondered if God still loves you?
Even when you turned your back
Saying I don't need God in my life
But His love you do not lack

Do you feel like His love
Just isn't meant for you?
Even though He loves you
No matter what you do

He loves you even when you sin
When you call upon His name
He listens and cares
For His love will always remain

He stretches out His arms
Asking you to come and stay
For He still loves you
Even when you think He's far away

It hurts Him to see you cry
It pains Him to see your sorrow
He wants to whisper in your ear
It'll be better tomorrow

You may feel like it'll last forever
But "sorrow will only endure for a night
For joy comes in the morning"
Then you'll know God's love is right

Inspired by Psalm 30:5

Trust Me

God says trust me
For He knows what's best for you
Even when you think
You're not going to make it through

He knows you can trust
When times are not tough
But He wants to know
If you can trust when times are rough

He wants to be in charge
For He knows the answer
So He asks you to trust Him
And completely surrender

He hates to see you worry
For He wants to help you
He tells you to trust
For He knows what to do

So just trust Him
That He will make a way
Let Him be in charge
Of each and everyday

Inspired by Isaiah 26:3-4 & Psalm 28:7

Just Pray

—⚜—

Just pray, when you feel all hope is gone
And it's so hard to carry on

Just pray, when everything's not going right
And you cry all through the night

Just pray, when life seems so unfair
And there doesn't seem to be anybody that will care

Just pray, when you've done all you can do
Feeling like you're not going to make it through

Just pray, laying your burdens down at Jesus's feet
Just take up His yoke, for "His yoke is easy and light"

Inspired by Matthew 11:30 & Mark 11:24

Dark Vs. Light Places in My Mind

———◦❀◦———

I was living in the darkest place in my mind
There was no light that I could see
I cried out and pleaded to God
Please don't let this place control me

Everywhere that I would go in my mind
The enemy had some lie keeping me in a bind
No peace or joy could I find

I wanted desperately to find the door
Out of this dark place
I looked for the door that would
Open me up to God's grace

I kept opening the doors of my past that always
Leads me back to a dark place in my mind
But every time I shut the doors to the past
When I look to the future what I seek I find

I find the place of peace in my mind
The tools I need to shut the door
To the dark place of negative thoughts I say
Your not welcome anymore

Mind Games

—◦⟨⟩◦—

The enemy loves to put negative thoughts in my mind
To try to use it as a playground
The enemy tries to convince me that hope
To win the mind game can't be found

The enemy had played with my mind for so long
That my mind had interpreted the truth as wrong

Now I've come to know what the enemy's lies are
I can choose what thoughts are true
I do not have to allow my negative thoughts
To control anymore of what I say or do

Maze

Life is like a maze
Every season is a different phase

In life there's all kinds of turns to make
You choose which one you take

Some turns turn into a mistake
Some turns turn into something great

Thinking turns into some kind of action
What turns you make shows your location

There's a way out of the maze thinking in your mind
Look to God for "what you seek you will find"

Inspired by Matthew 7:7

Fickle Feelings

You don't have to let your feelings be in control
Just don't give them that role

Feelings are so fickle
Their just unpredictable

Thank God He's the same yesterday, today and forever
So just knowing that doesn't it make you feel better

Tell your feelings you refuse to cater
You will always have to pay the bill for them later

If your hurt feelings want you to just run away
Just believe God will help so just stay and pray

You don't have to let your feelings cause you to react
The truth says you can have self control, so that's a fact

Your feelings are always temporary
Don't let them make you live in misery

Even when things don't go your way
You can still choose to have a good day

No matter what you feel
God's truth is always what's real

Inspired by Hebrews 13:8 & Galatians 5:23

I'm Not Alone

---※◈◈◈---

I feel so alone
Like I'm in a trapped room
Where there's nothing
But darkness and gloom

Its atmosphere is depressing
Where no one is there
My thoughts tell me
That no one cares

When I try to escape
I feel helpless in a way
Trying to go but
My thoughts want me to stay

It's like I'm a prisoner
For my thoughts have taken control
They influence what I'm feeling
My heart has a lonely hole

But when I reach out to God
Stretching forth my hands
He says in His word I'm not alone
For His word will always stand

Even when I feel all alone
Doesn't matter where I be
I can always call on God
For He is always here with me

Inspired by Joshua 1:9

Dear God

Tears are flowing on my checks
I feel so tired and weak

From all the pain and heartache
I feel it's more than I can take

I don't understand my purpose
Why was I created?
I know you see beyond my surface

I want to be home in heaven with you
Why do I go through what I do?

What's the reason you keep me here?
My heart has so much fear

I want to be a success
My life is just one big mess

Can you help me?
Open my eyes to see what you see

I know if you were ready for me to go
Then you would have taken me
But why right now are you saying no?

I feel so worthless and useless
I know you say not
to live by what I feel
But my pain
and heartache are real

Take this burden from me
Show me who you want me to be

I have so much uncertainty
So show me your reality

I'm pouring out my heart
I've completely fallen apart

Comfort and hold me
I command the devil to flee

I'm trying to have faith
So help me wait

I know you hear me when I cry
You've always helped
me to get by

Inspired by 2 Samuel
22:7 & Psalm 17:6

Heavy Heart

God my heart is heavy laden with pain and sorrow
You said "sorrow is for a night and joy will come tomorrow"

God I cry all day and through the night
You said my tears don't escape your sight

God I need you in my darkest hour
You said when I'm weak in you I have power

God wipe away my tears flowing like rain
You said your glory can be revealed through pain

God I feel as though all hope is gone
I must hope in the Lord to keep me strong

God I am restless and feel depressed
You said "come all who are heavy laden and I will give you rest"

Inspired by Psalm 56:8 & Matthew 11:28

My Cry to God

God, I cry out to you with everything within me
You said just trust in me and believe

God my trials seem like I just can't push through
You said I will help carry you

God my heart hurts deeply and all I do is weep
You said "those who sow in tears joy is what they reap"

God my heart has been torn apart
You said I can heal your broken heart

God I'm lost and have gone astray
You said just follow me I know the way

God I've fallen I need you to help me
You said I've given you grace and mercy

Inspired by Psalm 126:5

My Hearts Cry

—◦◦◦——

God hear my hearts cry
You help me to get by
Even when I don't understand why

God you are close to the broken hearted
"You'll finish in me what you've started"

God my heart, my everything
To you I surrender
So what You've promised me
God please remember

God give me rest within my soul
Fill me with your spirit till I'm full
Make my heart completely whole

For you God know the beginning to end
You can give me a heart mend
Thank you, that I can call you friend

God help me to listen to
What you have to say
Draw me back to you
When I go astray

God answer the prayers
Of the desires of my heart
Your word says you
Finish what you start

God remember all you said you would do
I believe your promises are true

Inspired by Psalm 34:18

Here I Am Again

God, here I am again
Once more at the place of brokenness
A place I've been many times before
Where I feel my emptiness

Hear my cry God
For I only want
To seek your face
To feel the warmth
Of your embrace

All I know to do
Is run back to you
Back to your arms of mercy
Though I feel so unworthy

Please hear my cry God
For you love to rescue
The brokenhearted
I believe your healing
Powers are unlimited

You still say to call you Father
You still call me your daughter

Inspired by Psalm 34:18

Midnight Prayer

God, let your peace wash away my tears
Let your peace calm all of my fears

I really desperately need you
Help me make it through

My heart is so heavy with sorrow
Let it be better tomorrow

I ask you to forgive my sin
Let me feel your joy again

This healing process is a journey
I'm weary and tired of hurting

I am serving others as your daughter
To please you, my heavenly father

Though evil and pain are real
I know a God who loves to heal

A God who understands
He wants us to put everything in His hands

While waiting God, help me to learn, grow and prepare
You said "You'd never give me more than I could bear"

Let all your promises in your word come true
I pray this prayer, humbling myself before you

Inspired by Psalm 29:11 & Isaiah 57:22

Release

At times I having a crying release
I then find my mind at ease
I open my heart to God's peace

Sometimes my feeling are overwhelming
They seem so overbearing

The battle of the mind is real
It affects how I feel

Yet ever time I cry out
Even when I'm filled with doubt

I can feel God calming my mind down
Telling me He still wears the victor's crown

Telling me to still wait on Him
Even when life looks dim

Telling me to not give up hope
To let Him help me cope

Telling me not to grow weary in doing what's right
To believe that He's already won the fight

Inspired by Matthew 27:29 & Galatians 6:9

God I Need You

—◦◦◦—

God I need you to help me rest tonight
I need you to tell me that it'll be alright
For right now I'm too tired and weak to fight

My head is clouded with so many doubts and fears
Please just let me feel your presence near
For my bed is very wet from all my tears

You say God in your Word not to doubt or fear
You say no matter what I feel You're always near

Help my mind be at ease so I can sleep in peace
Help the lies that I hear in my head to cease

Please help me and take these negative feelings away
Oh, please help me I desperately pray

Inspired by Mark 5:36

Rejoice

I praise God through the pain and rejoice
For happiness is not a feeling but a choice

I believe faith will make me completely whole
I'm taking back my joy the devil stole

Thoughts from the devil will tell me you have nothing to rejoice about
But I choose to believe God and rejoice anyways with a shout

Faith is believing in the unseen and the unknown
I choose to be happy for "I'll reap what I've sown"

There's more to rejoicing than just believing
Let my rejoicing show in my speaking

No matter what comes my way
I choose to speak life in what I say
I choose to rejoice in the Lord everyday

Inspired by Philippians 4:4

Miracles

———◆◆◆———

Miracles can happen
If you just believe
For God said "ask
And you shall receive"

Miracles are even hard to see
Our mind thinks how can that be?

It's hard to believe
That miracles happen everyday
It's hard to perceive
For God does the impossible in His own way

Inspired by Matthew 7:7

A New Day

I wake up to another day
I'm not sure what will come my way

If I can just focus on my future
Learning to become wiser

I have to believe I'm going to be all right
I just can't give up, I must fight

A new day is full of opportunities
There are so many possibilities

What I choose to do today
Will affect my life some way

For each day is like a climb
I take one step at a time

I need to have faith in what I can't see
Not let my past dictate what will be

I don't know what today may hold
But I will choose to be bold

Inspired by Ephesians 3:12

Live Life

I want to live life
Without holding back anything
To live my life with meaning

I want to live life
With a purpose
For I was designed
To worship

Though my life presently
Is not what I want it to be
I still believe in God
Who's inspired dreams in me

I'm still moving forward
Now I won't look back
There's nothing about my past
That causes me to lack

I'm pressing on
No matter how I feel
I'll keep believing
God's Word is real

The only way to live
Is to believe God is
And know
I'm a child of His

Inspired by Philippians 3:13

Champion

You can be a champion
Regardless of your past and what you've done
Because with God on your side you've already won

You can be strong just believe
Have faith in the unseen

Life can be hard and isn't fair
But don't let that keep you in fear

You can overcome abuse
Just don't let it be an excuse

Don't let falling down
Keep you on the ground

Your future will show
How much you let yourself grow

You can be a champion
Don't give up the fight
Always stand for what's right

Inspired by 1 Timothy 6:12

Mask Girl

She's always had to look perfect
So who she really was
No one could see

She just had such low self-esteem
That she didn't see her worth
In her true identity

She thought looking and acting perfect
Was the only way people accepted
And loved her and wanted her to be

Everyone thinks she's alright
Yet she cries herself to sleep at night

Everyone doesn't realize
That she is wearing a disguise

For her mask hides that she's broken within
Just hiding deep within her skin

She wears a mask so she won't feel
Rejection from people if she were to act real

Once she discovered her true identity in Christ
She surrendered being perfect
She loves who she is made to be
Now that girl is me

Inspired by Ephesians 2:10

Made by God

God you made me, so you can fix me
Help me to see what you see in me
To be all You created me to be

You are the Creator
There's nobody greater

I'm part of your creation
Your word is my foundation
Your my hope of salvation

Uniquely you made me
How you want me to be

You're the potter
I'm your daughter

So mold me to be
A vessel used by you
Help me to see
People from your view

I'm just the clay
Sometimes I go astray

When I do
Lead me back to you

I was made in your image
That's such a privilege

You formed me in my mother's womb
I am like a flower starting to bloom

"Fearfully and wonderfully"
God you made me

Inspired by Isaiah 64:8 & Psalm 139:14

Beautiful Butterfly

I started out as a caterpillar
Wanting to be an accomplisher

I crawled around the ground
Looking only down

I only survived thinking I was no one in particular
I didn't have a life that I thought was spectacular

I went into my shy cocoon
But it wasn't too soon

Before I turned into a beautiful butterfly
Learning that God was the only one who will satisfy

At first I didn't see the beauty within
I just saw my flaws and the ugliness of my sin

God opened up my eyes
To see past my disguise

I didn't think I would ever be worthy
God showed me that true beauty

Is about my hearts character
I don't have to have it all together

True beauty within will never fade
For God says I'm beautifully made

Inspired by Psalm 139:14

True Beauty

Beauty is not only skin deep
So why do we worry
About our outside
And not our soul to keep

We focus on and make
The outside look good
But the inside
Is what really should

We think our looks
Is all that shows
From our head
To our toes

But in fact God "see's our heart"
Who we are from the very start

Inspired by 1 Samuel 16:7

The Unknown

As I embark into the unknown
I only know what God's shown

The unknown gives my heart such fear
For I don't know if I'll reach my goals and get there

I just don't know when or where
But God is always near

I don't know how to get to
What God has for me in the future
But God says "I have great plans for you"
In His scripture

The unknown can be uncomfortable to go through
But God says He will help guide you

You cannot always see what lies ahead
But just remember what God said

Inspired by Jeremiah 29:11 & Philippians 1:6

In the Waiting

In this time of waiting my faith is often shaken
My dreams look at times like they have been taken

My future doesn't look clear
I don't know if I'll be able to get there

I choose to trust God though my future isn't clear to see
Even when the storms of life look like they'll overtake me

I choose to believe God has a great future planned for me
I'm just uncertain on what His future plan will be
But I wait and trust though I can not see

Inspired by Psalm 56:3-4

Life Choices

What am I going to do
With my life starting today
Am I going to go my own way
Or go God's way

What am I going to choose
If I go my own way my life I'll loose

What do I want to portray
For the world to see
Am I going to let them
See the God in me?

Every choice I make
Affects my future to be

So God I want to give
You total control
For in this story of life
Gods given me a role

He has a purpose for my life
That He wants me to walk out
For putting Him first and serving others
Is what life's all about

It's my life, it's my choice
What am I going to do?
God says "to choose life more abundantly"
Each day His mercies are new

Inspired by John 10:10

God's Will

Lord, I know right now
I'm going through a season
Through my hardships
I don't always see the reason

Lord, help me to learn
To be patient, waiting on you
Even when it seems
It's all I can stand to do

Lord, I don't want to miss out
On what you have for me
In this time of waiting
My future I can't clearly see

Lord, I trust and put my hope in you
You see my future
You know what I'm going to do

Lord, lead my way
Into your predestined will
I will wait on you until

You show me
My next step to take
For it's all for
Your names sake

Inspired by John 7:17 & Hebrews 10:36

REFERENCES

1. Baby Jesus on page 3: Refer to Luke 2:1-20
2. My Savior on page 4: Refer to John 3:16
3. God on page 5: Refer to Matthew 28:19
4. God's Friend on page 6: Refer to 1 Corinthians 10:13
5. First Love on page 7: Refer to John 4:14
6. Love Is on page 8: Refer to 1 Corinthians 13:4-7
7. Hope is on page 10: Refer to Gal 6:8; Romans 8:25
8. Be Humble on page 11: Refer to Proverbs 16:18
9. I Still Love You on page 12: Refer to Psalm 30:5
10. Trust Me on page 13: Refer to Isaiah 26:3-4 & Psalm 28:7
11. Just Pray on page 14: Refer to Matthew 11:30 & Mark 11:24
12. Maze on page 17: Refer to Matthew 7:7
13. Fickle Feelings on page 18: Refer to Hebrews 13:8,Titus 1:8 & Galatians 5:23
14. I'm Not Alone on page 19: Refer to Joshua 1:9
15. Dear God on page 20-21: Refer to 2 Samuel 22:7 & Psalm 17:6
16. Heavy Heart on page 22: Refer to Psalm 56:8 & Matthew 11:28
17. My Cry to God on page 23: Refer to Psalm 126:5
18. My Heart's Cry on page 24: Refer to Psalm 34:18
19. Here I Am Again on page 25: Refer to Psalm 34:18
20. Midnight Prayer on page 26: Refer to Psalm 29:11 & Isaiah 57:22
21. Release on page 27: Refer to Matthew 27:29 & Galatians 6:19
22. God I Need You on page 28: Refer to Mark 5:36
23. Rejoice on page 29: Refer to Philippians 4:4
24. Miracles on page 30: Refer to Matthew 7:7
25. A New Day on page 31: Refer to Ephesians 3:12
26. Live Life on page 32: Refer to Philippians 3:13
27. Champion on page 33: Refer to 1 Timothy 6:12
28. Mask Girl on page 34: Refer to Ephesians 2:10
29. Made By God on page 35: Refer to Psalm 139:14 & Isaiah 64:8
30. Beautiful Butterfly on page 36: Refer to Psalm 139:14
31. True Beauty on page 37: Refer to 1 Samuel 16:7
32. The Unknown on page 38: Refer to Philippians 1:6
33. In the Waiting on page 39: Refer to Psalm 56:3-4
34. Life Choices on page 40: Refer to John 10:10
35. God's will on page 41: Refer to John 7:17 & Hebrews 10:36

Printed in the United States
by Baker & Taylor Publisher Services